better together*

*This book is best read together, grownup and kid.

 akidsco.com

a kids
book
about

a kids book about

alopecia

by Bergson Van

a
kids
book
about

Printed in the United States of America.

A Kids Book About books are available online: *akidsco.com*

To share your stories, ask questions, or inquire about bulk
purchases (schools, libraries, and nonprofits), please use
the following email address: *hello@akidsco.com*

Print ISBN: 978-1-958825-27-3
Ebook ISBN: 978-1-958825-28-0

Co-authored with Karen Lee
Designed by Rick DeLucco
Illustrative elements by Bergson Van
Edited by Emma Wolf

To my mom and dad for loving and guiding me
while always allowing me to choose my path
on this alopecia journey.

To my brother, Ollie, for loving me just as I am.

And to Hamsty and Turtley, just because.

Intro

• • • • •• • • • •• •

Alopecia can be a scary thing. The cause varies by individual, and there's no cure in most cases. Kids with alopecia can lose self-esteem just when they are learning to build it.

Alopecia is more common than you think. But we haven't seen it, heard about it, or talked about it much. Until now. People like Ayanna Pressley and Viola Davis are just a couple of the brave individuals who have created space for others by sharing their hair-loss journeys. Now is the time to celebrate our differences. Bald is bold and beautiful.

Grownups, let's empower those with alopecia by letting them know that they aren't alone. Let's normalize alopecia, such that we *all* truly believe that hair doesn't define beauty. And to grownups of kids *with* alopecia: everything will be OK; your little one is more resilient than you can imagine!

Hi, my name is Bergson. I love dinosaurs, hamsters, Minecraft, and playing video games.

By the way, I also have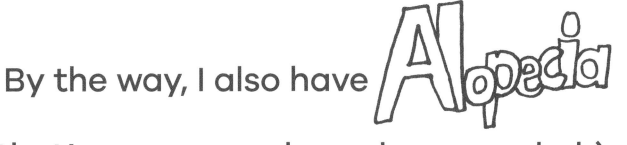

(that's pronounced aaa-low-pee-shuh).

Alopecia means your hair falls out.

Some people call it hair loss.

Alopecia can mean having a few bald patches or losing **ALL** of your hair, sometimes even including your eyebrows and eyelashes.

Some or all of the hair can come back, but you might lose it again.[1,2,3]

[1] Lauren C. Strazzulla et al., "Alopecia Areata," Journal of the American Academy of Dermatology 78, no. 1 (January 2018): pp. 1-12, https://doi.org/10.1016/j.jaad.2017.04.1141.
[2] Dimitra Aikaterini Lintzeri et al., "Alopecia Areata – Current Understanding and Management," JDDG: Journal Der Deutschen Dermatologischen Gesellschaft 20, no. 1 (January 2022): pp. 59-90, https://doi.org/10.1111/ddg.14689.
[3] Jerry Shapiro and Maria Hordinsky, ed. Jeffrey Callen and Abena O Ofori, n.d., "Evaluation and Diagnosis of Hair Loss," accessed March 22, 2023.

That's what happened to me.

Having alopecia can be difficult because it means you have to protect your head from the sun, your head gets too hot too quickly, and some people may need to wear a hat, headscarf, or a wig all day.

For example, on a hot day,
I usually feel *waaay* hotter than
everyone else, and on a cold day,
I usually feel *waaay* colder.

When I was a little boy, what bothered me most was not being able to explain my alopecia.

I had a **hard** time with the questions people asked me and being stared at all the time.

My mom said my classmates and friends just wanted to understand what was happening to me.
They were curious.

So, during Alopecia Awareness month in September, my mom came to my class to explain alopecia, and for that one day, I went to school and didn't cover my head.

It felt good
to share
my story.

It felt great
to just
be me!

There are many reasons alopecia can happen.

It can be caused by medications, stomach issues, mold, and other things.[4,5]

[4]Shapiro and Hordinsky, "Evaluation and Diagnosis of Hair Loss."
[5]Strazulla et al., "Alopecia Areata," 1–12.

Some people think it is caused by stress, or the foods people eat, or it's genetic.[6,7]

[6]Shapiro and Hordinsky, "Evaluation and Diagnosis of Hair Loss."
[7]Strazulla et al., "Alopecia Areata," 1–12.

There are lots of scientists
working to figure out
why alopecia happens!

What I understand is that
it's different for everyone.

I don't know why I have alopecia.

But I do know that, for me, my alopecia works just like allergies.

When someone has allergies to, say, pet hair, they will sneeze or cough because something is there that just doesn't belong and their body is trying to get rid of it.

For MY alopecia, my body thinks my hair shouldn't be there, so it tries to get rid of all of it.*

*This is called an autoimmune response.

Alopecia is no one's fault.

Alopecia can happen to anyone
and at any time.

My parents tell me some people think that kids who identify as female need to have hair in order to be beautiful.

I know that's not true, but not everyone does.

In fact, having no hair can be really beautiful.

Some people don't have hair for reasons different from my own:

- They lose their hair from taking certain medications.

- They lose their hair as they get older—all over, or just in some places.

- They choose to have no hair and remove it by cutting or shaving it off, maybe because they like it or because they want to support someone they know who doesn't have hair.*

*That's called solidarity!

My mom thinks dealing
with alopecia for the first time
may actually be easier
for kids than it is for grownups.

I believe it !

When I was little, I thought hair falling out was "normal" because that's all I knew.

My little brother, Ollie, only knows me without hair.

It took 5 years to feel at peace
with where I am today.

And to me, right now, there
is no worst part of alopecia.

For example...

I never have to
which I think

get my hair cut, is great!

I have friends who support me when people say mean things about my alopecia or ask me questions about it.

It helps to know that I have friends, family, and teachers who are there for me and who love me for who I am.

In the past, whenever someone said something unkind to me, I always felt that something was wrong with me.

My body doesn't respond that way anymore. I feel OK about having alopecia. It's just a part of who I am!

When someone says something unkind, I tell myself, "That's *their* problem, *not* mine."

I usually have a few
responses ready to say so I
am mentally prepared.

I stay really, really calm. Talking it out with someone I trust helps me stay calm.

And I've actually started something new where I take what a person says as a compliment, not an insult.

And it works!

My mom and dad say
I'm brave for sharing my story.

But I'm just writing this book because there are some important things I'd like you to know.

grownups:

- There are many reasons why someone can lose their hair.

- No hair may not be a bad thing.
  (It may actually make us stronger inside!)

- Some people are actually OK with not having hair.

- And if you have a kid with alopecia, it's going to be OK.

For kids who don't have alopecia:

- Be kind and don't laugh when you see someone who looks different than you.

- Know how people with alopecia feel when you do laugh (hint: it doesn't feel good).

- Not having hair isn't who I am, it's just one part of me (see note about dinosaurs!).

For kids with alopecia:

- Nothing is wrong with you.

- Anyone can lose hair.

- You can cover your head, if you want to. And if you're comfortable, you can decide not to cover up anymore!

I know people with hair
may not understand what
it's like to be without hair.

Right now, I don't have hair and it's actually OK for me.

It's nothing to be afraid of if you choose to just let it be.

Maybe someday I'll understand why I have alopecia, or maybe even try to change it.

But right now, that's not what's most important to me.

My mom and dad said if I
ever change my mind, we
can figure it out together.

Everyone has something difficult they are going through; for me, you can see it (that's my alopecia).

But for most people you cannot see what they are having a hard time with.

We are all different,
but also the same.

Besides, being different
doesn't have to be a bad thing.

Even if I still wear a cap every day, I know people can see that I have alopecia.

And maybe one day I will be comfortable enough to go without my cap.

But for now, I'm happy to just be . . . . .

..................me.

Outro

● ● ● ● ● ● ● ● ● ●

The medical community has only scratched the surface with new medications to reverse hair loss, and health care plans have begun to catch up to cover related costs. What can you and your kid do to help build empathy and acceptance around alopecia?

- Start a campaign and proudly wear blue in September for Alopecia Awareness month.

- Enjoy media with your kid which features characters without hair: *Harold and the Purple Crayon*, *Popeye*, or Vision and Nebula (Marvel characters). Did lack of hair influence their amazing adventures or how cool they are?

- Consider being a pen pal to build community and a sense of belonging. These organizations are just a few who can make the connection: **National Alopecia Areata Foundation**, **Children's Alopecia Project**, and **Alopecia UK**.

Wouldn't it be fantastic if we normalized alopecia, and everyone hiding under a hat or a wig could just be themselves every day? Imagine the freedom for everyone involved. Just imagine!

About The Author

Bergson Van (he/him) is just like his peers, but he's the only one with alopecia. Since Bergson began his alopecia journey, his family has been right beside him all the way, through ups, downs, and a whole lot of uncertainty.

Over time, Bergson found a way to navigate this personal challenge and decided to share his story with hopes that others who are like him can relate and feel heard, and that their grownups know that all will be OK. Additionally, this book is a reminder for those who have hair to practice empathy and be kind.

Bergson's mom, Karen Lee (she/her), focuses her time on teaching Bergson about the science behind and strategies to manage both alopecia and mental health while always spreading awareness and promoting acceptance.

 @a_kids_alopecia_book   f   Facebook.com/AKidsAlopeciaBook

a kids book about MONEY
by Adam Stramwasser

a kids book about BEING INCLUSIVE
by Ashton Mota & Rebekah Bruesehoff

a kids book about diversity
by Charnaie Gordon

a kids book about LEADERSHIP
by Orion Jean

a kids book about SAFETY

by Soraya Sutherlin, CEM
in partnership with JUDY

a kids book about CLIMATE CHANGE
by Zanagee Artis
Olivia Greenspan

a kids book about IMAGINATION
by LEVAR BURTON

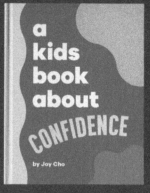
a kids book about CONFIDENCE
by Joy Cho

a kids book about ANXIETY
by Ross Szabo
The Mind Behind Happy Faces

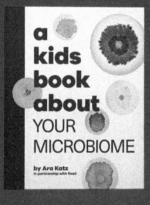
a kids book about YOUR MICROBIOME
by Ara Katz
in partnership with Seed

a kids book about racism
by Jelani Memory

a kids book about DISABILITIES
by Kristine Napper

a kids book about

a kids book about DIVORCE
by Ashley Simpo

a kids book about cancer
by Dr. Kelsie Storm & Sarah Porter

a kids book about BEING TRANSGENDER
by Gia Parr
in partnership with The GenderCool Project

a kids book about DEPRESSION
by Kileah McIlvain

a kids book about shame

a kids book about THE TULSA RACE MASSACRE